Greek Americans

Nichol Bryan

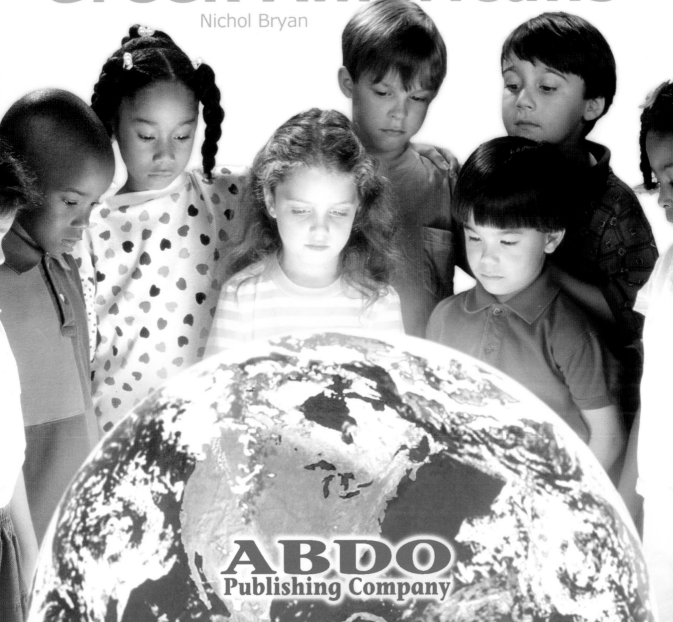

ABDO
Publishing Company

visit us at
www.abdopub.com

Published by ABDO Publishing Company, 4940 Viking Drive, Edina, Minnesota 55435.
Copyright © 2004 by Abdo Consulting Group, Inc. International copyrights reserved in all countries. No part of this book may be reproduced in any form without written permission from the publisher.

Printed in the United States.

Cover Photo: Corbis
Interior Photos: AP/Wide World pp. 24, 29; Corbis pp. 1, 2-3, 7, 8, 10, 11, 12, 14, 16, 17, 19, 22, 25, 27, 30-31; Getty Images p. 28; Kayte Deioma pp. 5, 21, 23

Series Coordinator: Jennifer R. Krueger
Editors: Kristianne E. Buechler, Kate A. Conley
Art Direction & Maps: Neil Klinepier

All of the U.S. population statistics in the One Nation series are taken from the 2000 Census.

Special thanks to Professor Theofanis Stavrou at the University of Minnesota for help with the Greek language.

Library of Congress Cataloging-in-Publication Data

Bryan, Nichol, 1958-
    Greek Americans / Nichol Bryan.
        p. cm. -- (One nation)
    Includes bibliographical references and index.
    Summary: Provides an overview of the religion and culture of Greek Americans and presents some information on the history of the Greek people.
    ISBN 1-59197-527-1
      1. Greek Americans--Juvenile literature. [1. Greek Americans. 2. Immigrants.] I. Title.

E184.G7B79 2004
973'.04893--dc22
                                           2003062811

Contents

Greek Americans 4

Ancient Land 6

Odyssey 12

Becoming a Citizen 18

Colorful Culture 20

Greek Gifts 26

Glossary 30

Saying It 31

Web Sites 31

Index 32

Greek Americans

Ever since Christopher Columbus discovered America, people around the world have been coming to the country. Columbus was an Italian explorer working for Spain. He discovered the Americas in 1492. Since then, millions of people have left their home countries to discover America.

Many of these **immigrants** came for the same reasons. They came from poor countries and needed money. They heard of fortunes to be made in America. Some immigrants came to escape war. Many wanted to practice their religion freely. Most of all, they wanted their families to be safe.

Immigrants from Greece have come for all of these reasons. They came with high hopes but were sometimes disappointed. However, many immigrants found safety and success in the New World. Along the way, they have become an important part of American **culture**.

*Opposite page: **Many Greek Americans honor their heritage by wearing traditional clothing for celebrations.***

Ancient Land

Greece is a land of mountains and islands. The main part of the country juts out of southeastern Europe. It is surrounded by the Aegean, Mediterranean, and Ionian seas. Its territory also includes more than 2,000 islands.

Greece was not always a unified country. It used to be a collection of powerful **city-states**. These city-states began to develop 5,000 years ago. Greek city-states such as Athens and Sparta became great commercial centers. They were also dominant military powers.

About 2,500 years ago, the **culture** of the Greek city-states flourished. The Greeks created temples and public buildings of incredible beauty. Great thinkers such as Pythagoras began to explore mathematics and science. Philosophers such as Socrates and Plato developed ideas for government.

Most importantly, the Greeks devised a new political system. In this system, people cast votes to determine who would rule. Two thousand years later, the Greek idea of **democracy** inspired the founders of America.

But for Greece, this golden age would not last. Greece was conquered by the Roman Empire in 146 BC. The Romans greatly admired Greek **culture**. They adopted many Greek ideas, technologies, and artistic styles.

One of the most famous buildings of ancient Greece is a temple in Athens called the Parthenon.

In 1827, the Greeks and the Turks fought in the Battle of Navarino. It was a decisive battle in the Greek fight for independence.

In the AD 400s, Rome fell, too. Greek territory became part of the Byzantine Empire. For the next 1,000 years, the Byzantine Empire ruled these lands.

Greek lands fell into the hands of the Ottoman Empire in 1453. This empire was based in what is now Turkey. The Ottomans ruled Greece for almost 400 years.

The Ottomans left Greece after the Greeks waged a war of independence for seven years. Greece was supported by France, the United Kingdom, and Russia. The Greeks won their independence in 1829.

At this time, Greece became a **constitutional** monarchy. In this system, a king or queen must follow a constitution. The countries that liberated Greece appointed foreign-born kings for the country. The people of Greece worked to create a peaceful, independent nation. But, two world wars lay ahead of them.

In 1917, Greece joined the **Allies** in **World War I**. The Allies won the war in 1918. Because of this, Greece gained more territory from the Ottoman Empire.

The king of Greece at this time was George II. In 1923, he was forced from the throne by people who wanted Greece to be a **republic**. Greece became a republic the next year. But, the revolts continued.

King George II regained the throne in 1935. However, he was not the only one with power in Greece. **Communists** were also gaining power in the government. And in 1936, the king allowed General Ioannis Metaxas to establish a military **dictatorship**.

In 1940 and 1941, Greece was invaded by Italy and Germany. This was during **World War II**. The Greek people suffered terribly under German occupation. King George II returned to the throne again in 1946. But, there was more suffering ahead for the Greek people.

The fighting of World War II led to a **civil war** in Greece. In this war, Greek communists **rebelled** against the royal government.

Greek soldiers march during the Greek Civil War.

It was a long, difficult war for the people of Greece. The **communist rebels** were defeated in 1946. A royal government was re-established. Luckily, brighter times lay ahead for the Greek people.

The 1950s were a somewhat stable time for Greece. The **economy** was improving. Uncertainty in the government remained, however. In 1967, there was another military revolt, and a **dictatorship** was once again established.

Finally in 1974, a group of military officers overthrew the dictatorship. This allowed the people of Greece to once again create a **democratic republic**. The country has remained a democracy ever since.

Today, economic development has started to make life better for the citizens of Greece. With peace and stability, few Greeks **immigrate** every year to the United States. But, this was not always the case.

Today, Greece has a strong economy. It has its own stock exchange where stocks and bonds are sold.

Odyssey

The first Greek **immigrants** came to America even before it was a nation! They settled in present-day Florida in the 1760s. They were trying to escape the violence and uncertainty in their homeland. Many Greeks died during the voyage. Many also died after arriving at this first settlement.

Other small groups of Greeks came to the United States in the early 1800s. These early Greeks also struggled to survive. They suffered the same **prejudice** that other immigrant groups in America faced. Still, they worked hard to succeed.

Throughout the 1800s, the continuing violence in Greece drove many Greeks to immigrate to the United States. Most Greeks had been poor farmers or fishers in their native land. Warfare and

The *Odyssey*

Around 700 BC, the Greek poet Homer wrote about the journeys of a hero named Odysseus. The poem was called the *Odyssey*. The *Odyssey* tells of Odysseus's long journey home after fighting in the Trojan War. He travels for ten years by sea, looking for his homeland. Many Greek immigrants remembered this tale as they made their long journey across the Atlantic to America.

The Journey from Greece to the United States

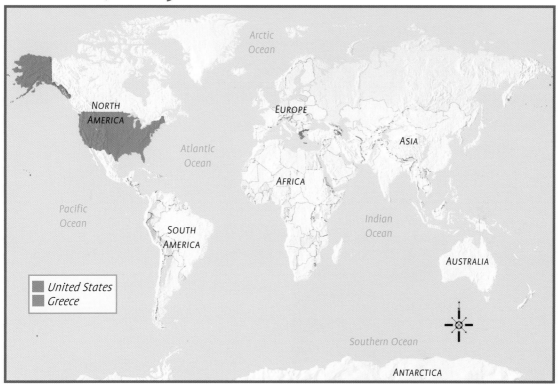

political strife made their lives even harder. After hearing of opportunities in America, many Greek peasants **immigrated**.

Greeks began to come to the United States in large numbers in the 1890s. The main wave of Greek immigrants came between 1890 and 1921. In 1891, there were only 2,500 Greeks in America. However by 1922, between 300,000 and 500,000 Greeks had settled in the United States.

At first, Greeks coming to the United States were mostly men. Many came to earn enough money to help their families in Greece get out of debt. But, many more found it hard to earn enough to help their families. Still, by the mid-1900s, women and entire families were crossing the Atlantic to America.

Greeks often settled in communities where other Greeks lived. Chicago was the final stop for many of these **immigrants**. Thousands of Greeks came to a neighborhood on the city's west side. This neighborhood became known as Greektown. Many Greek businesses and restaurants are still located there.

Like many other European immigrants, thousands of Greeks settled in New York. This city was a major port of entry for ships coming across the Atlantic. Today, New York has more Greek Americans than any other state.

Many Greek immigrants in New York took classes to learn English.

Greek-American Communities

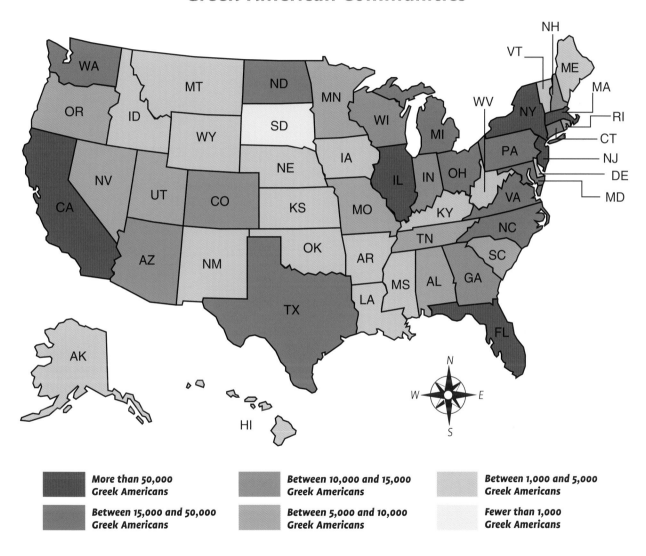

Legend:

- More than 50,000 Greek Americans
- Between 15,000 and 50,000 Greek Americans
- Between 10,000 and 15,000 Greek Americans
- Between 5,000 and 10,000 Greek Americans
- Between 1,000 and 5,000 Greek Americans
- Fewer than 1,000 Greek Americans

15

Boys pose in front of a Greek coffee shop, one of many businesses started by Greek immigrants.

Good jobs were not easy to come by for many Greek **immigrants**. Few of them spoke English. They brought farming and fishing skills from their villages in Greece. But, these skills were of little use in the industrial cities of America.

By living in Greektowns, however, these newcomers learned to be successful. They started their own aid societies and Greek-language newspapers. They also began the first Greek Orthodox churches in the United States.

Many of the first Greek Americans had to take unskilled jobs. But, some hardworking Greeks started restaurants, coffee shops, markets, and other businesses. Soon, they were helping new Greek **immigrants** get established. Many immigrants urged their children to take advantage of educational opportunities in America.

Meanwhile, conditions improved in Greece toward the end of the twentieth century. Immigration to the United States slowed. But, the close-knit Greek communities continued to grow and succeed. Today, there are around 1 million Greek Americans living in the United States.

Saint John's Greek Orthodox Church is one of the many churches started by Greek immigrants in New York.

Becoming a Citizen

Greeks and other **immigrants** who come to the United States take the same path to citizenship. Immigrants become citizens in a process called naturalization. A government agency called the United States Citizenship and Immigration Services (USCIS) oversees this process.

The Path to Citizenship

Applying for Citizenship

The first step in becoming a citizen is filling out a form. It is called the Application for Naturalization. On the application, immigrants provide information about their past. Immigrants send the application to the USCIS.

Providing Information

Besides the application, immigrants must provide the USCIS with other items. They may include documents such as marriage licenses or old tax returns. Immigrants must also provide photographs and fingerprints. They are used for identification. The fingerprints are also used to check whether immigrants have committed crimes in the past.

The Interview

Next, a USCIS officer interviews each immigrant to discuss his or her application and background. In addition, the USCIS officer tests the immigrant's ability to speak, read, and write in English. The officer also tests the immigrant's knowledge of American civics.

The Oath

Immigrants approved for citizenship must take the Oath of Allegiance. Once immigrants take this oath, they are citizens. During the oath, immigrants promise to renounce loyalty to their native country, to support the U.S. Constitution, and to serve and defend the United States when needed.

Sample Questions from the Civics Test

How many stars are there on our flag?

What is the capital of the state you live in?

Why did the Pilgrims come to America?

How many senators are there in Congress?

Who said, "Give me liberty or give me death"?

What are the first 10 amendments to the Constitution called?

In what month do we vote for the president?

Why Become a Citizen?

Why would an immigrant want to become a U.S. citizen? There are many reasons. Perhaps the biggest reason is that the U.S. Constitution grants many rights to its citizens. One of the most important is the right to vote.

U.S. Department of Justice
Immigration and Naturalization Service

Print clearly or type your answers using CAPITAL letters. Failure to print clearly may delay your application. Use blac

Application fo

Part 1. Your Name *(The Person Applying for Naturalization)*

A. Your current legal name.

Family Name *(Last Name)*

Write your INS "A"- nu

A _ _ _ _ _ _ _

Given Name *(First Name)*

Full Middle Name *(If applicable)*

FOR INS US

Bar Code

B. Your name exactly as it appears on your Permanent Resident Card.

Family Name *(Last Name)*

Given Name *(First Name)*

Full Middle Name *(If applicable)*

C. If you have ever used other names, provide them below.

Family Name *(Last Name)*

Given Name *(First Name)*

Middle Name

Colorful Culture

It was difficult for many Greek Americans to adjust to their new homeland. However, they have a strong **culture**. They carried on traditions with their families, food, faith, and language. To this day, Greek Americans have a colorful culture to be proud of.

Keeping Family Close

Traditional Greek families tended to be large and very close. Parents, children, grandparents, uncles, and aunts all lived together. Fathers were considered the head of the family. Women were expected to marry and then live with their husbands' family. Having lots of children was a sign of a successful marriage.

Greeks who came to America worked to preserve their traditional family structure. Many Greek Americans today, however, live in smaller families. And, women often work outside the home. However, many traditions in Greek-American families still exist.

Opposite page: Dancing is a popular part of Greek-American culture. These dancers perform at an annual Greek festival in Long Beach, California.

A Lively Culture

Greek Americans continue to celebrate a **culture** that is lively and full of hospitality. Family gatherings are usually large affairs. They include traditional Greek songs and dances such as the *hasapiko* and the *kalamatiano*. Greek Americans also enjoy modern, popular songs from Greece.

Traditional Greek food includes many fruits and vegetables such as olives, tomatoes, and cucumbers.

Food and Family

Food is important in Greek **culture**. For the Greeks, food is a way to bind the family together. It is also a way to show hospitality to strangers.

Several traditional Greek dishes are popular today in the United States. One is called moussaka. It is a dish similar to lasagna. Baklava is another traditional Greek food. It is a sweet, flaky dessert made from ground nuts and honey. Many Americans go to Greek restaurants to enjoy these and other Greek foods.

People of Faith

Almost all Greeks, and most Greek Americans, belong to the Greek Orthodox Church. This is a branch of the Eastern Orthodox Church. They practice many of the same rites that other Christians practice. The Orthodox Church also celebrates familiar Christian holidays such as Christmas and Easter.

Not all Greek Americans follow this faith. Some have chosen other faiths or are not religious. For many Greek Americans, though, faith is an important part of their lives.

Greek Orthodox churches are often beautifully decorated inside and out.

23

The Language of Learning

At this immersion school in Florida, the teacher speaks Greek, and the Greek alphabet hangs on the wall.

Greek is one of the oldest European languages. It is also an influential language. For example, many of the terms used in science and math are based on the Greek language. Also, many of the words we use in English can be traced back to Greek.

Many Greek Americans don't want their children to forget their ancestral language. That is why many Greek-American communities have started their own schools. In these schools, children learn to speak Greek. They also learn about Greek **culture**.

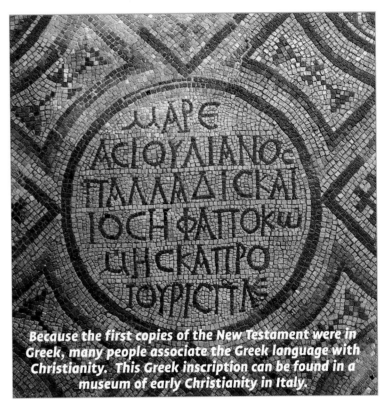

Because the first copies of the New Testament were in Greek, many people associate the Greek language with Christianity. This Greek inscription can be found in a museum of early Christianity in Italy.

The Greek Alphabet

The word *alphabet* comes from the first two letters of the Greek alphabet. These are alpha (A) and beta (B). Some of the 24 letters in the Greek alphabet look familiar. Other Greek letters, such as sigma (Σ) and omega (Ω), are not so familiar. Scientists and mathematicians around the world still use these Greek letters as symbols in their formulas.

Greek Gifts

Greek Americans have made many significant contributions to America. Greek **immigrants** and their descendants have especially made big contributions to politics and **culture** in the United States.

Many Greek Americans have served in public office. Michael Dukakis, former governor of Massachusetts, is the son of Greek immigrants. Dukakis was elected to the Massachusetts House of Representatives in 1962. He became governor in 1975. He even ran for president, losing to George H.W. Bush in 1988.

Two political commentators, George Stephanopoulos and Arianna Huffington, are a frequent sight on television. Stephanopoulos grew up in Cleveland, Ohio. He was the son of a Greek Orthodox priest. He first gained national attention as one of President Bill Clinton's advisers. Today, he hosts his own television show called *This Week*.

Michael Dukakis

Arianna Huffington moved from Greece at the age of 16. She now makes her home in Los Angeles, California. Besides being a television commentator and newspaper columnist, she ran for governor of California in 2003.

Nia Vardalos

Another famous Greek American on television is Nia Vardalos. She was the star of the television series *My Big Fat Greek Life*. The series was based on her hit film, *My Big Fat Greek Wedding*. Both the television show and the film celebrated what it is like to belong to a Greek-American family.

Greek Americans have also contributed to the business world. William Stavropoulos is the son of Greek **immigrants**. He started working with Dow Chemical Corporation in 1967 as a research chemist. Dow Chemical is a leading science and technology company. He was named president and chief executive officer of the company in 1995.

The Greeks who came to America's shores have faced adversity with hard work and determination. They have become full members of American society. But, they have also preserved a proud and unique **culture**.

Arianna Huffington

Glossary

allies - people or countries that agree to help each other in times of need. During World War I, the United States, Great Britain, France, and Russia were called the Allies.

city-state - a state consisting of a city and its surrounding territory.

civil war - a war between groups in the same country.

communism - a social and economic system in which everything is owned by the government and is distributed to the people as needed.

constitution - the laws that govern a country.

culture - the customs, arts, and tools of a nation or people at a certain time.

democracy - a governmental system in which the people vote on how to run their country.

dictator - a ruler with complete control who usually governs in a cruel or unfair way.

economy - the way a nation uses its money, goods, and natural resources.

immigration - entry into another country to live. A person who immigrates is called an immigrant.

prejudice - hatred of a particular group based on factors such as race or religion.

rebel - to disobey an authority or the government.

republic - a form of government in which authority rests with voting citizens and is carried out by elected officials, such as those in a parliament.

World War I - from 1914 to 1918, fought in Europe. The United States, Great Britain, France, Russia, and their allies were on one side. Germany, Austria-Hungary, and their allies were on the other side.

World War II - from 1939 to 1945, fought in Europe, Asia, and Africa. The United States, France, Great Britain, the Soviet Union, and their allies were on one side. Germany, Italy, Japan, and their allies were on the other side.

Saying It

baklava - BAH-kluh-vah
George Stephanopoulos - JOHRJ stehf-uh-NAWP-uh-lihs
hasapiko - hah-SAH-pee-koh
Ioannis Metaxas - yaw-AHN-yees met-ahk-SAHS
kalamatiano - kah-lah-ma-teh-an-OH
moussaka - moo-SAH-kuh
Nia Vardalos - NEE-uh vahr-DAH-lohs
Pythagoras - puh-THAG-uh-ruhs
Socrates - SAHK-ruh-teez

Web Sites

To learn more about Greek Americans, visit ABDO Publishing Company on the World Wide Web at **www.abdopub.com**. Web sites about Greek Americans are featured on our Book Links page. These links are routinely monitored and updated to provide the most current information available.

31

Index

A
Aegean Sea 6
Athens 6
Atlantic Ocean 14
B
Bush, George H.W. 26
Byzantine Empire 9
C
Chicago, Illinois 14
citizenship 18
civil war 10, 11
Cleveland, Ohio 26
Clinton, Bill 26
Columbus, Christopher 4
D
dance 21
discrimination 12
Dukakis, Michael 26
F
family 4, 14, 17, 20, 21, 22, 25, 28
Florida 12
food 20, 22
France 9

G
George II (king of Greece) 9, 10
Germany 10
Greektowns 14, 17
H
Huffington, Arianna 26, 28
I
independence (Greek) 9
Ionian Sea 6
Italy 4, 10
L
language 16, 17, 20, 24, 25
Los Angeles, California 28
M
Massachusetts 26
Mediterranean Sea 6
Metaxas, Ioannis 10
music 21
N
New York City, New York 14
O
Ottoman Empire 9

P
Plato 6
Pythagoras 6
R
religion 4, 17, 20, 23, 26
Roman Empire 7, 9
Russia 9
S
Socrates 6
Spain 4
Stavropoulos, William 28
Stephanopoulos, George 26
T
Turkey 9
U
United Kingdom 9
United States Citizenship and Immigration Services 18
V
Vardalos, Nia 28
W
World War I 9
World War II 10